A Jewish Cookbook for Children

illustrated by Sonja Glassman

JULIAN MESSNER ◐ NEW YORK

A Jewish Cookbook for Children

by Ronnie Steinkoler

For Alex, Manya, Danny, Jeremy
Sweetness and love

ACKNOWLEDGMENTS

I wish to extend my gratitude to the late Ziporah Kosoff of the Board of Jewish Education for confirming my ideas about the need for a Jewish cookbook for children.

Much appreciation goes to the people at Bank Street College who have helped in many ways. This cookbook is a reflection of the feelings we share about the needs of growing children.

I offer love and thanks to Alex Steinkoler and Nancy Steinthal for their support, inspiration, ideas, and editing.

Thank you to all my family for their love and patience.

Copyright © 1980 by Ronnie Steinkoler
All rights reserved including the right of
reproduction in whole or in part in any form.
Published by Julian Messner, a Simon & Schuster
Division of Gulf & Western Corporation, Simon &
Schuster Building, 1230 Avenue of the Americas,
New York, N.Y. 10020.

JULIAN MESSNER and colophon are trademarks of Simon & Schuster, registered
in the U.S. Patent and Trademark Office.

Manufactured in the United States of America

Design by Elizabeth Woll

Library of Congress Cataloging in Publication Data

Steinkoler, Ronnie.
   A Jewish cookbook for children.

    SUMMARY: Introduces basic cooking techniques and recipes for a variety of traditional Jewish dishes.
    1. Cookery, Jewish—Juvenile literature.
[1. Cookery, Jewish] I. Glassman, Sonja.
II. Title.
TX724.S74   641.5'676   80-17428
ISBN 0-671-33093-4

Contents

INTRODUCTION   8
IN THE BEGINNING...   9
RULES FOR COOKING   11
PREPARATION   12
TABLE OF STANDARD
  MEASUREMENTS   13
MEASURING AND ASSEMBLING   14
COOKING TERMS   15
UTENSILS FREQUENTLY USED   17
SHABBAT   20
   Challah   21
   Egg Noodle Dough   26
   Apple Noodle Pudding   27
   Chicken Soup   28
   Roast Chicken   31
   Stuffing   32
   Coleslaw   34
   Fresh Fruit Salad   35
   Fruit Compote   36
   Sponge Cake   37
   Egg Kichel   39
   Rolled Sugar Cookies   41

ROSH HASHANAH   43
    Apples with Honey   43
    Honey Cake   44
    Tzimmes   46
YOM KIPPUR   48
    Cinnamon Rolls   49
SUCCOTH   51
    Candied Apples   52
HANUKKAH   54
    Potato Pancakes   55
    Applesauce   56
TU BI-SHEVAT   58
    Baked Apples   59
PURIM   60
    Hamantashen   61
    Brownies   64
PASSOVER (PESACH)   66
    Maror   68
    Charoset   68
    Karpas   69
    Lamb Bone   70
    Hard Boiled Eggs   70
    Potato Pudding   72
    Matzoh Balls   73
    Matzoh Brie (Fried Matzoh)   74
    Sponge Cake   76

    Almond Macaroons   77
INDEPENDENCE DAY   79
    Hummus   80
    Tahina   82
    Falafel   83
    Kibbutz Salad   84
    Pita   86
SHAVUOT   89
    Butter   89
    Whipped Cream   90
    Egg Salad   90
    Tuna Fish   91
    Rice Pudding   92
    Cheesecake   94
    Lemonade   96

Introduction

When I was a little girl, I used to bake with my mother. I remember the feel of the dough as I pushed it into shapes with my rolling pin. I remember the smell of baking sugar cookies filling the house with their sweet aroma. I remember the excitement I felt when I took my very own cookies out of the oven and served them later for dessert.

Such memories are very special to me. For many years, I have been cooking with my children. Now I want to share these experiences with other young people who I hope will have much joy from them.

Jewish cooking has been around since the Biblical times of Abraham and Sarah (the first Jewish ancestors). Each of the Jewish holidays and festivals is associated with special foods. Many of the recipes in this book have been handed down for hundreds, or even thousands, of years from great grandmothers to grandmothers to mothers and now to you. Although great grandfathers might not have taken part in cooking, there is no reason why boys of today cannot start to enjoy it.

The recipes are chosen and arranged so most of them can be done without adult help. The few which require help are starred.

Almost all the recipes in this book use fresh ingredients which are usually available in local stores. Few canned foods are used. No preservatives or artificial additives are recommended.

In the Beginning...

Jewish cooking is almost 6,000 years old. From the Bible we learn that Sarah and Abraham welcomed visitors to their home with curd*, milk, bread and fine cakes. They prepared food for company just as we do today. Hospitality, then as now, is an important part of the Jewish tradition.

Nowadays, when we sit down to dinner, we talk about the day's events. Sometimes we tell jokes.

*like the lumps in cottage cheese

Sometimes, on a holiday, we sing songs. In ancient times, families enjoyed these very same things. In some ways we are very much alike.

How different was the food in ancient times from the food on our table today? In those days, people drank milk, ate cooked cereal, eggs, grapes, raisins, apples, dates, nuts, melons, onions, cucumbers, fish and meat much as we do today. They used salt and pepper and garlic and ginger to season their food. Honey, instead of sugar, was used as a sweetener.

Today, we have a greater variety of foods, many more kitchen tools for preparing them, many more ways of preserving food and keeping it fresh, and a great many more recipes from which to choose. Jewish cooking has been influenced by the cooking of the different countries throughout the world in which the Jewish people have lived. For instance, *falafel* has its origins in the Middle East while noodles (*lokshen*) originated in the Eastern European countries.

According to Jewish dietary law, all meat, fish and poultry must be *kosher*. In other words, no meat or meat products may be cooked or served with milk or any other dairy products. However, certain foods are considered *parve*—those which may be served with either meat or dairy. *Parve* foods are eggs*, fish (those with backbone, fins and scales), vegetables, vegetable oil, fruits, and breads and pastries made without dairy or meat products. *Kosher* wine and

---

*Eggs which have blood spots are not kosher. When using eggs, break each one into a cup, one at a time, then transfer it to a bowl. This way, eggs with blood spots are easily discarded.

whiskey are also *parve*. All recipes in this cookbook are in accordance with Jewish dietary laws.

Along with recipes, each section is devoted to one of the major holidays. Each holiday has its special foods which serve to remind us of the history of our ancestors. On Passover, for example, we eat *matzoh* or unleavened bread. Yeast-raised bread takes time to rise and the Jews, who were being chased by the Egyptians, had no time to wait. Dipping apples in honey on *Rosh Hashanah* is a symbolic gesture of hope for a "sweet year." Purim's treat is *hamantashen*, a three-cornered pastry representing the three-pointed hats worn by the Jews of Ancient Persia.

Each recipe is bound up with Jewish history and tradition. This inheritance will add a special flavor to your cooking.

Rules for Cooking

These rules help make cooking easy, enjoyable and safe. Many of them may already be familiar.

CLEANLINESS

Wash hands before working with food.
Use aprons to keep clothes from getting dirty.
If you have long hair, tie it back.
Keep work areas and utensils clean.
Clean up after cooking.

CAREFULNESS AND SAFETY TIPS

Cut with sharp edge of knife pointed away from you.
Cut on cutting boards so as not to scratch counter or table tops.
Use pot holders to handle hot pots and hot baking dishes.
Turn pot handles toward the center of the stove to avoid bumping into them or catching them in your clothes.
Use a trivet under a hot pot or dish to prevent it from burning the counter or table top.

KEEPING KOSHER

Make sure all foods are *kosher*. Meat and dairy are never mixed.
Meat and dairy utensils and dishes are kept separate from each other.
Parve foods can be used with either meat or dairy.

Preparation

Read recipe thoroughly.
Assemble ingredients and utensils beforehand.
Measure ingredients beforehand.

In recipes for cakes and cookies, exact measurements are very important because dry and liquid ingredients must be in proper proportion to insure fine texture, moistness or crispness, and proper rising. Cooking soups and salads is not as exacting, so if you prefer more of one ingredient, you can add it to your dish. There is a lot of room for experimenting.

Cooking terms are important since they are unique to cooking and might not be familiar. The cooking terms used in this book are on pages 15-17.

Difficult recipes are starred at the top of the page and at the point where you might need adult help.

Table of Standard Measurements

Dash or pinch = $1/8$ teaspoon
1 teaspoon = $1/3$ tablespoon
1 tablespoon = 3 teaspoons
2 tablespoons = $1/8$ cup
4 tablespoons = $1/4$ cup
5 $1/3$ tablespoons or 16 teaspoons = $1/3$ cup
8 tablespoons = $1/2$ cup
16 tablespoons = 1 cup
1 cup = $1/2$ pint
2 pints = 1 quart
4 quarts = 1 gallon

COMMON FOOD EQUIVALENTS

8 tablespoons = 1 stick of butter or margarine
1 stick of butter or margarine = 1/2 cup
1/2 pint cream = 2 cups whipped
1 pound cottage cheese = 2 cups
4 to 6 eggs = 1 cup
1 pound all-purpose flour = 4 cups
1 pound cake flour = 4 1/2 cups
1 pound sugar = 2 cups
1/2 cup honey = 1 cup sugar in sweetness
1 pound raisins = 2 cups packed

Measuring and Assembling

To measure an ingredient, you need the proper utensil as well as a place to put the ingredient after it is measured. You may use wax paper, aluminum foil, plates, cups, glasses, bowls or any containers to hold the ingredients until you are ready to use them.

Cooking Terms

BAKE   to cook in the oven
BASTE   to pour liquid over food, especially meat, during cooking
BEAT   to mix ingredients with a fork, eggbeater or mixer
BLEND   to mix ingredients until smooth
BOIL   to cook a liquid in a pot on the top of the stove until bubbles appear all over the surface
BROIL   to cook under the heating element in the oven
BROWN   to cook until the color of the food becomes brown
BRUSH   to brush lightly using a pastry brush
CHOP   to cut food into small pieces with a knife or chopper
COMBINE   to add one ingredient to another and mix
CREAM   to make shortening or butter light and fluffy by beating
DICE   to cut food into little pieces or cubes
DOT   to place small pieces of an ingredient over the top of another food
DRAIN   to let the liquid run off
FLOUR   to sprinkle flour over surface
FOLD   to mix ingredients lightly
FRY   to cook in a frying pan over heat, usually with oil or shortening

Garnish   to decorate one food with another

Grease   to rub a pan, casserole or baking dish with oil, shortening, butter or margarine so it is evenly coated

Knead   to mix dough by hand. Put dough on clean, flat surface which has been lightly floured. With the heels of your hands push down into the dough as though you were pushing it away from you. Fold dough over. Turn it around a quarter circle. Repeat this process until dough is smooth and elastic, not sticky.

Mash   to beat solid food with a masher until it becomes light and fluffy

Melt   to change a solid to a liquid by heating it

Mince   to chop or cut into tiny pieces

Mix   to stir ingredients together

Peel   to remove outer skin or layer of foods such as oranges, apples

Proof   to make sure yeast is active by mixing it with sugar and water. When it foams it is active.

Roast   to cook meats and poultry in the oven

Roll   to flatten dough with a rolling pin or roll into a log or ball or roll one ingredient in another

Sauté   to fry over a low flame in oil or shortening

Separate   For example, to separate the yolk from the white of an egg: Crack the egg against the side of a bowl, making sure, as the shell is opened, that the yolk stays in one half of the shell. Gently pour the yolk from one half of the shell to the other half so the white falls into the bowl. Place yolk in separate dish.

Shred   to cut food into thin strands using a grater
Sift   to put dry ingredients through a sifter
Simmer   to cook over a low flame so liquid that rises to the top begins to bubble but does not boil
Skim   to remove unnecessary matter that rises to the top of a liquid
Stir   to blend in ingredients, using a circular motion
Strain   to put foods through a strainer which will remove lumps, seeds, etc. so that the result will be fine or clear
Toss   to mix lightly
Whip   to beat rapidly with a beater or whisk in order to increase volume

Utensils Frequently Used

MEASURING

Measuring cup for liquids
Set of measuring cups for dry measure: $1/4$, $1/3$, $1/2$, 1 cup quantities
Measuring spoons: $1/4$, $1/2$, 1 teaspoon, 1 tablespoon

PREPARATION

Bowls: small, medium, large
Rubber spatula
Knives
Wooden spoons
Kitchen forks
Large metal spoon
Slotted spoon
Pancake turner
Potato masher
Vegetable peeler
Apple corer

Grater
Food chopper
Ladle
Cutting board
Juicer
Wooden chopping bowl
Cake tester
Cookie cutters
Melon ball scoop
Scissors
Tongs

Blender (you can use a grater instead)
Wax paper
Aluminum foil
Strainer
Sifter
Colander

Plastic bags
Eggbeater
Rolling pin
Pastry brush
Electric mixer

COOKING

Pot holders
Saucepans with lids
Double boiler with lid
Frying pans with lids
Dutch oven with lid
Roasting pan
V-rack for roasting
Cookie sheets
Muffin pans
Round cake pans (8 or 9 inches)
Assorted casserole pans
Tube pans
Racks for cooling
Trivets
Toaster
Springform Pan (a pan whose sides or rim are fastened to the pan's bottom by a clamp or spring)
Candy thermometer

Many of these pots and pans can be substituted for each other.

Shabbat
(The Jewish Sabbath)

Shabbat is a very special day of the week. It begins at sundown on Friday night and ends at sundown on Saturday. During that time, Jewish people do not work because, according to the Bible, after creating the world, God rested on the seventh day—*Shabbat*. Special ceremonies and rituals make up the day. It is a day of peace.

Today, as for the past 5,000 years, women and girls welcome *Shabbat* by lighting candles and saying a prayer. The men say *kiddush* (a blessing) over the wine and bless the *challahs* as well.

In many homes, the table is set with the best tablecloth, china and silver. Special foods are prepared beforehand so no work will be done on *Shabbat*.

The following recipes are for foods typically served on *Shabbat*. Many of the foods are served on other holidays and festivals as well.

CHALLAH *(Parve)*

Challah is the traditional bread served on *Shabbat* and on all other holidays except Passover. It is a yeast bread which is made with eggs, and it is usually braided.

On *Shabbat,* the loaves are served whole. Most of the time, they have poppy seeds to remind us of the *manna* the Jews received from God when they were crossing the desert after the exodus from Egypt. *Manna* is the white, flaky edible food that was found on the ground by the Israelites during the exodus. It was regarded by them as a gift from God. The *manna* appeared to have poppy seeds in it.

When the *challah* dough is being prepared for baking, a small piece is removed and burned. This is called separating the *challah*. It is a tradition from ancient times, when a portion of bread was reserved for the priests in the Temple. To symbolize the fact that twelve loaves were given to the priests, the *challah* is usually braided with six strands. Since there are two loaves served on *Shabbat*, six plus six equals twelve. To make it easier to handle, you can make three-strand *challahs*.

On the holidays of *Rosh Hashanah* and *Yom Kippur*, round *challahs* are served to symbolize a full year of blessings. Sometimes, on *Yom Kippur*, a ladder is braided onto the top of the *challah* to signify that on this day a person should serve God with all his or her strength—to reach the greatest height of perfection. On *Purim*, *challahs* are shaped in the form of a triangle similar to the shape of the hats worn in this ancient time. (See the section on *Purim*.)

Since it is easier to knead a small amount of dough at one time, this recipe may be cut in half.

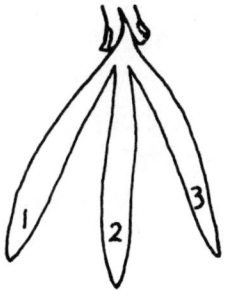

1. Roll out 3 strips (like rolling clay cigars).

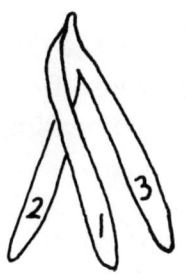

2. Pinch 3 ends together.

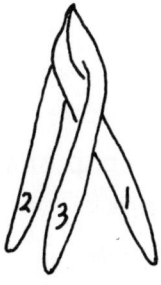

3. Fold strip #1 over strip #2.

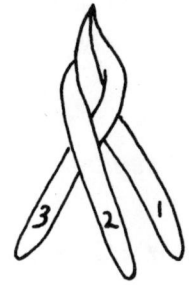

4. Fold strip #3 over strip #1.

5. Continue braiding, then pinch ends of dough together.

INGREDIENTS: ASSEMBLE AND MEASURE
7 1/2 cups all purpose flour
    plus flour for kneading
4 packages dry yeast
1/4 cup sugar
1 tablespoon salt
1/4 cup oil
    plus oil for greasing bowl
    and baking sheet
3 eggs
1 egg yolk
1 tablespoon poppy seeds
2 1/2 cups warm water

UTENSILS: ASSEMBLE
1 set measuring cups
1 measuring cup for liquid
1 large spoon
1 measuring tablespoon
1 very large bowl
1 fork
1 pastry brush
1 small bowl
1 baking sheet
1 dish towel
1 rack
flat surface for kneading

WHAT TO DO

Dissolve   yeast with sugar in 1/2 cup of water (This is called proofing).

Let stand   10 minutes, until it foams

Beat   3 eggs lightly in bowl

Add   { oil, salt, 2 cups water, yeast mixture } to eggs

Add   flour, 1 cup at a time, to egg mixture until all flour is used

Knead   on lightly floured board for 10 minutes until dough is smooth and elastic

Grease   large bowl

Put	dough into bowl
Turn	dough over so it is covered with oil
Cover	bowl with cloth
Let rise	in a warm place for 1½ to 2 hours until twice original size
Punch	down dough
Separate	*challah*
Divide	*challah* into loaves
Braid	*challah*
Grease	baking sheet
Arrange	loaves on baking sheet
Let rise	until twice original size
Beat	egg yolk plus one teaspoon water
Brush	*challah* with egg mixture using pastry brush
Sprinkle	poppy seeds on *challahs*
Put	loaves into cold oven
Turn	oven on to 425° for 10 minutes
Lower	oven temperature to 350°
Bake	for about 45 more minutes on middle rack. To test if *challah* is done, tap it with the handle of a knife. It should sound hollow.
Remove	*challah* from oven
Cool	on rack

Makes 2 large or 3 medium Challah

EGG NOODLE DOUGH (*Parve*)

This dough can be used to make noodles of any size or shape. It can be used in a pasta machine, but it is more fun to roll the dough and cut the noodles oneself. The noodles can be used immediately or stored for future use. Noodles can be part of many dishes. They are delicious when cut narrow (fine) for soups or wide (broad) for noodle pudding. After they are cooked in boiling water, they can be eaten plain or with a pat of butter or cottage cheese.

INGREDIENTS: ASSEMBLE AND MEASURE
3 1/2 cups all-purpose flour
4 eggs

UTENSILS: ASSEMBLE
1 one-cup measuring cup
1 large bowl
1 knife
1 rolling pin
1 large metal rack
clean, flat surface

WHAT TO DO

Put	3 cups flour into bowl
Add	eggs
Mix	dough with hands until smooth
Divide	dough into thirds
Roll out	1/3 with rolling pin into thin, flat sheet
Cut	dough into strips of desired length and width
Lay	strips of dough on metal rack to dry
Repeat	with remaining dough
Use	immediately or store in canister

Makes about 1 pound of dough

APPLE NOODLE PUDDING (*Parve*)   *Help

Either homemade or store-bought noodles are used for this recipe.

INGREDIENTS: ASSEMBLE AND MEASURE
8 ounces wide noodles
1/2 cup cooking oil
4 eggs
1/2 cup sugar
1 teaspoon cinnamon
1/4 teaspoon nutmeg
1/4 teaspoon salt
1/2 cup seedless raisins
3 medium apples (washed)
3 quarts water

UTENSILS: ASSEMBLE
1 large pot
1 colander
1 measuring cup
1 set measuring spoons
1 cutting board
1 medium knife
1 apple peeler
1 large bowl
1 fork
1 9" x 13" baking dish

WHAT TO DO

Preheat	oven to 350°
Pour	water and salt into pot
Bring	water to a boil
Pour	noodles into pot
Wait	for water to boil again
Lower	flame to medium
Cook	for 8 minutes on medium heat
*Pour	noodles into colander
Drain	in sink
Peel	apples
Cut	apples into thin slices

27

Beat	eggs with fork in bowl
Mix	{ noodles, eggs, oil } in bowl
Add	{ cinnamon, nutmeg, salt, sugar, apples, raisins } to noodles
Stir	until thoroughly mixed
Grease	baking dish
Pour	mixture into baking dish
Bake	in 350° oven for 45 minutes
Serve	hot or cold
Store	covered in refrigerator

Serves 4-6

CHICKEN SOUP   *Help

This soup is often served on Friday nights and holidays as well. It can be served with egg noodles or *matzoh* balls.

People always joke about serving chicken soup to someone who is sick. Perhaps that's because mothers and grandmothers always say, "What, you don't feel well? Let me make you some chicken soup and you'll feel much better."

INGREDIENTS: ASSEMBLE AND MEASURE

1 clean chicken whole or cut into eighths (about 4 pounds)
3 quarts cold water
2 carrots (washed)
2 stalks celery (washed)
2 sprigs parsley (washed)
1 tablespoon salt
1/2 teaspoon pepper
2 medium onions

UTENSILS: ASSEMBLE

1 large pot with lid
1 vegetable peeler
1 knife
1 large wooden spoon
1 slotted spoon
1 set measuring spoons
1 measuring cup
1 strainer
1 large bowl
1 plate

WHAT TO DO

Put   chicken pieces into pot with water
Simmer   over low flame
Skim   matter that rises to the top after

soup has been simmering for 15 minutes, and again after soup has been cooking for 1/2 hour. Use wooden spoon.

Peel	{ carrots onions
Slice	{ carrots celery onions
Add	{ sliced carrots sliced celery sliced onions parsley salt pepper } to soup
Cover	pot
Simmer	1 1/2 hours
Remove	{ chicken carrots } with slotted spoon
Put	on plate
* Pour	soup through strainer into bowl
Remove	carrots from strainer
Add	carrots to soup
Reheat	soup to serve
Store	covered in refrigerator

Serves 4 to 6

ROAST CHICKEN　　　　　　　　　　　　　　　　　　*Help

This is a traditional main course for Shabbat. It is served on many other holidays as well. It is delicious served with stuffing.

INGREDIENTS: ASSEMBLE AND MEASURE
1 (4 to 5 pound) roasting chicken (cleaned)
2 teaspoons salt
½ teaspoon pepper
½ teaspoon thyme
2 teaspoons paprika
1½ cups water

UTENSILS: ASSEMBLE
1 measuring cup
1 set measuring spoons
1 roasting pan
1 V-shaped rack
paper towels
small skewers and string, if stuffing is used
1 spoon
1 pair tongs or large fork

WHAT TO DO

Preheat	oven to 350°
Rinse	chicken: inside and outside
Pat	chicken dry with paper towels
Rub	{ salt, pepper, thyme } over inside and outside of chicken
Stuff	cavity, using spoon
Insert	skewers across opening
Tie	string tightly around skewers and legs
Sprinkle	paprika over outside of chicken

Place	chicken on rack in roasting pan
Pour	water into bottom of pan
Roast	in 350° oven 25 minutes per pound (with stuffing, 20 minutes per pound) Multiply amount of pounds x number of minutes per pound.
*Turn	chicken over to brown on other side when half-done, using tongs
Remove	from oven
Serve	hot or cold
Store	wrapped in foil in refrigerator

Serves 4 to 6

STUFFING (*Parve*)

There are many different types of stuffing. This is a basic recipe which goes well with everything. On Passover, matzoh crumbs can be substituted for bread crumbs.

Because stuffing spoils quickly, it should be placed in the chicken just before roasting. Always remove stuffing before storing chicken. Wrap the stuffing separately and store it in the refrigerator.

INGREDIENTS: ASSEMBLE AND MEASURE	UTENSILS: ASSEMBLE
5 cups bread crumbs	1 medium knife
1 medium onion	1 large frying pan
1 stalk celery (washed)	1 set measuring cups

½ cup parve margarine
½ teaspoon salt
¼ teaspoon pepper
1 teaspoon poultry seasoning
1 tablespoon chopped parsley (washed)
⅓ cup water
2 eggs

1 set measuring spoons
1 large bowl
1 large wooden spoon
skewers and string
cutting board

WHAT TO DO

Peel	onion	
Dice	{ onion, celery }	
Melt	margarine in frying pan over low heat	
Saute	onion and celery until soft, but not brown	
Mince	parsley	
Combine	{ salt, pepper, poultry seasoning, minced parsley, bread crumbs, eggs }	in bowl
Add	{ onion mixture, water }	to bread crumb mix
Spoon	stuffing into chicken cavity	
Sew	cavity with skewers and string	
Tie	legs together with string	

Enough stuffing for a 5-pound chicken

COLESLAW (*Parve*)

Coleslaw is a side dish. It is frequently served at a *Shabbat* afternoon *kiddush*, but since it goes well with many dishes, it can also be served at other times.

INGREDIENTS: ASSEMBLE AND MEASURE
1 head of cabbage, medium (washed)
2 carrots (washed)
1 small green pepper (washed)
1 small onion
½ cup mayonnaise
2 teaspoons lemon juice
1 teaspoon salt
1 teaspoon sugar

UTENSILS: ASSEMBLE
1 vegetable peeler
1 medium knife
1 large wooden spoon
1 measuring cup
1 set measuring spoons
1 grater
1 large bowl
1 cutting board

WHAT TO DO

Peel	carrots
Cut	cabbage into quarters
Cut	green pepper into large chunks
Peel	onion
Cut	onion in half
Grate	carrots, cabbage, green pepper, onion — into bowl using coarse side of grater

Add	⎧ mayonnaise ⎨ lemon juice ⎨ salt ⎩ sugar
Toss	with vegetables
Serve	cold
Store	covered in refrigerator

Serves 6

FRESH FRUIT SALAD (*Parve*)

INGREDIENTS: ASSEMBLE AND MEASURE
Use any fresh fruit in season
   in any combinations

12 fruits = 8 servings

apples	plums
pears	nectarines
oranges	apricots
grapefruits	kiwi fruit
tangerines	(Chinese
ugli fruit (tangelos)	gooseberries)
bananas	mangoes
grapes	papaya
berries	cherries
melons	pineapples
peaches	

1/3 cup sugar or
    3 tablespoons honey
1 tablespoon lemon juice

UTENSILS: ASSEMBLE
1 measuring cup
1 measuring tablespoon
1 medium knife
1 large bowl
1 wooden spoon
1 cutting board
1 melon ball scoop
   (for melons)

WHAT TO DO

	Wash	fruit
	Remove	stems, pits, and skin unfit to eat
	Cut	fruit with knife into bite-size pieces on cutting board
	Combine	all fruit in bowl
	Stir in	{ honey or sugar lemon juice
	Refrigerate	until served cold

Serves 8

FRUIT COMPOTE (*Parve*)

This dish can be served either cold or hot.

INGREDIENTS: ASSEMBLE AND MEASURE
½ pound prunes
½ pound dried apricots
½ pound dried pears
½ cup raisins
¾ cup sugar
3 tablespoons orange juice
¾ cup water

UTENSILS: ASSEMBLE
1 measuring cup
1 measuring tablespoon
1 colander
1 medium wooden spoon
1 9" x 9" baking dish

WHAT TO DO

Preheat	oven to 325°	
Rinse	{ prunes, apricots, pears }	in colander under running water
Drain	fruit	
Arrange	{ prunes, apricots, pears, raisins }	in baking dish
Sprinkle	sugar	
Pour	{ orange juice, water }	over fruit
Bake	in 325° oven 1 hour	
Remove	from oven	
Cool	compote	
Store	in refrigerator	

Serves 6

SPONGE CAKE (*Parve*)

This cake is often served at a *kiddush*. It is delicious with fresh fruit such as strawberries. If the cake is made in two layers, you can use the layers for a strawberry shortcake.

INGREDIENTS: ASSEMBLE AND MEASURE

8 eggs
1½ cups sugar
1½ cups all-purpose flour
½ teaspoon baking soda
1 teaspoon salt
½ cup orange juice
1 teaspoon vanilla
¼ cup powdered sugar

UTENSILS: ASSEMBLE

1 eggbeater or mixmaster
1 small bowl
1 large bowl
1 set measuring spoons
1 set measuring cups
1 spatula
1 10" tube pan or
    2 8" round, layer pans
wax paper
1 cake rack

WHAT TO DO

Preheat	oven to 350°
Separate	egg yolks from whites
Beat	{ egg whites with ½ cup sugar } until stiff
Beat	egg yolks with 1 cup sugar
Add	{ vanilla, salt } to egg yolk mixture
Beat	until lemon yellow
Blend in	flour and orange juice, first one and then the other by turns
Fold	egg whites into mixture
Fit	wax paper into pan as liner
Bake	in 350° oven on middle rack for 1 hour
Remove	cake from oven

Turn	pan upside down on rack
Cool	on rack
Loosen	cake from sides of pan
Remove	cake gently from pan
Remove	wax paper from cake
Sprinkle	with powdered sugar
Store	wrapped in foil or plastic

Makes a 10" tube cake

EGG KICHEL (*Parve*)

The word *kichel* means a small cake. More than one is *kichlach*.

INGREDIENTS: ASSEMBLE AND MEASURE	UTENSILS: ASSEMBLE
2 cups all-purpose flour	1 set measuring cups
3/4 teaspoon baking powder	1 flour sifter
3/4 teaspoon salt	1 fork
3 eggs	1 small knife
1/3 cup super-fine sugar	1 rolling pin
flour for rolling dough	1 medium bowl
	1 large bowl
	1 cookie sheet
	1 rack
	1 metal spatula

WHAT TO DO

Preheat	oven to 350°
Sift	flour, baking powder, salt — together
Beat	eggs with fork
Add	eggs to flour mixture
Knead	flour-egg mixture for 5 minutes
Flour	flat surface lightly
Roll out	dough to about 1/4" thickness
Cut	dough into 3" shapes such as diamonds, squares, rectangles, circles, etc.
Flour	cookie sheet lightly
Arrange	cookies on cookie sheet about 1/2" apart
Bake	at 350° on center rack of oven for 1/2 hour until lightly browned
Remove	from oven
Remove	from sheet with metal spatula
Cool	on rack
Serve	when cooled
Store	in closed container

About 4 dozen cookies

ROLLED SUGAR COOKIES (*Parve*, if made with *parve* margarine)

INGREDIENTS: ASSEMBLE AND MEASURE
2½ cups all-purpose flour
1 teaspoon baking powder
½ teaspoon salt
½ cup butter or margarine
1 teaspoon vanilla
2 eggs
flour for rolling dough
butter or margarine for
    greasing baking sheets

UTENSILS: ASSEMBLE
1 set measuring spoons
1 set measuring cups
1 electric mixer
1 large bowl
1 spatula, metal
1 spatula, rubber
1 rolling pin
1 knife
1 (or 2) cookie sheets
cookie cutters
1 rack
wax paper

WHAT TO DO

Preheat	oven to 425°
Sift	{ flour, baking powder, salt } together
Cream	butter or margarine in electric mixer
Add	brown or white sugar to butter mixture
Add	eggs and vanilla to butter-sugar mixture
Beat	well
Add	sifted dry ingredients

Blend	thoroughly
Divide	dough in half
Wrap	in wax paper
Refrigerate	overnight

Roll	on floured surface with rolling pin to ¼" thickness
Cut	into shapes with cookie cutters
Grease	cookie sheets
Bake	in 425° oven about 7 minutes until light brown
Remove	from oven
Remove	from cookie sheet with metal spatula
Cool	on rack
Store	in closed container

About 6 dozen cookies

Rosh Hashanah

Rosh Hashanah, the Jewish New Year, is one of the holiest days of the year.

Rosh Hashanah means "head of year." It not only starts the new year off, it also begins ten days of "repentance," which end with *Yom Kippur*, the holiest day of the year. (*See* the next holiday section.) It is during these ten days that God judges everyone.

Although *Rosh Hashanah* is a very serious day, it is not a sad one. It is a time of new hope.

On this holiday, it is symbolic to serve sweets with wishes for a *"Shana Tova,"* a good year. Dipping slices of apple and pieces of *challah* in honey, serving *tzimmes* (a sweet carrot pudding) and honey cake are meant to insure a year of sweetness.

As on *Shabbat*, the table is set with the best china, silver and tablecloth. Everything is beautiful for a Happy New Year.

APPLES WITH HONEY (*Parve*)

INGREDIENTS: ASSEMBLE AND MEASURE
4 medium apples (washed)
½ cup honey

UTENSILS: ASSEMBLE
1 knife
1 measuring cup
1 apple corer
1 small bowl
1 plate

WHAT TO DO

Core	apples
Slice	apples into halves, then quarters, then eighths
Pour	honey into small bowl
Arrange	apple slices around dish of honey

Serves 12

HONEY CAKE (*Parve*)

Honey cake is traditionally served on *Rosh Hashanah*. It is also a popular dessert on *Shabbat* and other holidays as well.

INGREDIENTS: ASSEMBLE AND MEASURE	UTENSILS: ASSEMBLE
2¾ cups all-purpose flour	1 measuring cup
2 teaspoons baking soda	1 set measuring spoons
2 teaspoons baking powder	2 large bowls
½ teaspoon salt	1 electric mixer
1 cup sugar	1 rubber spatula
1 cup honey	1 flour sifter
3 eggs	1 9" x 5" loaf pan
½ cup oil	1 metal rack
1 cup coffee (use instant)	
2 teaspoons vanilla	
oil for greasing baking pan	

WHAT TO DO

Preheat	oven to 325°
Beat	eggs with honey in mixer
Add	sugar to egg mixture
Mix	baking soda with coffee
Mix	{ baking soda-coffee mixture oil vanilla egg mixture
Sift	{ flour salt baking powder
Add	flour mixture to egg mixture gradually
Grease	baking pan with oil
Bake	in 325° oven on middle rack for 1 hour
Remove	from oven
Cool	on rack
Remove	from pan
Cool	thoroughly
Serve or Wrap	in foil to store

Makes a 9" loaf cake

TZIMMES (Parve)

Tzimmes, a carrot pudding, has its origins in Eastern Europe. There are many variations and combinations of ingredients for this dish.

INGREDIENTS: ASSEMBLE AND MEASURE	UTENSILS: ASSEMBLE
8 medium carrots (washed)	1 knife
2 medium sweet potatoes or 1 small 8 ounce can	1 vegetable peeler
½ cup brown sugar	1 measuring cup
½ cup orange juice	1 set measuring spoons
½ teaspoon salt	1 medium pot with cover
¼ cup margarine	1 slotted spoon
½ cup water	1 9" x 9" baking dish
margarine to grease pan	1 cutting board
	aluminum foil

WHAT TO DO

Peel { carrots / fresh sweet potatoes

Slice { carrots / fresh sweet potatoes

Cook { carrots / fresh sweet potatoes } in salted water / in covered pot / over low heat / until tender / (20 minutes)

Preheat   oven to 350°
Grease   baking dish

Remove	{carrots, sweet potatoes}	from pot with slotted spoon so liquid will drain
Arrange	{carrots, sweet potatoes}	in baking dish
Pour	orange juice over carrot-sweet potato combination	
Sprinkle	brown sugar over carrot-sweet potato combination	
Dot	with margarine	
Cover	with aluminum foil	
Bake	in 350° oven for 50 minutes	
Serve	hot	
Store	cool, covered, in refrigerator	

Serves 4 to 6

Yom Kippur

Yom Kippur, the Day of Atonement, is the holiest day of the year. It is a day on which we ask God's forgiveness for our sins. Jews all over the world gather in their synagogues to pray. Prayers are begun with *Kol Nidre,* a special prayer for this day.

Fasting starts before the first prayers on the eve of *Yom Kippur.* The blowing of the *shofar* (ram's horn) on the eve of the following day marks the end of the fast. Everyone, except children, fasts.

To prepare for the fast, it is important not to eat or drink anything salty or spicy which makes people thirsty.

After the fast, it is customary to have a light meal. Cakes and sweets, which are lightly spiced with cinnamon and flavored with honey, are popular for breaking the fast. They are usually served with a glass of juice.

CINNAMON ROLLS

INGREDIENTS: ASSEMBLE AND MEASURE
3 cups self-rising cake flour
1/8 teaspoon salt
2/3 cup milk
1/4 cup butter plus 1 tablespoon
1/2 cup sugar
1 teaspoon cinnamon
1/2 cup raisins
1/2 cup chopped walnuts
butter for greasing baking sheets
flour for rolling dough

UTENSILS: ASSEMBLE
1 set measuring cups
1 set measuring spoons
1 flour sifter
1 small saucepan
1 large bowl
1 small bowl
1 rolling pin
1 wooden spoon
1 (or 2) baking sheets
1 pastry brush

WHAT TO DO

Preheat	oven to 400°	
Sift	{ flour, salt }	into bowl
Melt	butter in saucepan	
Mix	{ flour-salt, 1/4 cup melted butter, milk }	until smooth
Roll	dough on lightly floured surface until 1" thick	
Brush	dough with 1 tablespoon melted butter	

Sprinkle	{ nuts raisins ¼ cup sugar cinnamon }	all over dough
Roll	dough into jelly-roll log	
Cut	into 1" slices (swirls)	
Grease	baking sheet	
Arrange	rolls, swirl side flat, on baking sheet 1½" apart	
Sprinkle	rolls with ¼ cup sugar	
Bake	12 to 15 minutes in 400° oven	
Serve	hot or cold	
Store	in plastic bag or wrapped in foil	

About 24 rolls

Succoth

Succoth is a nine-day celebration of the fall harvest. Huts which are called *sukkas* are built outdoors. These symbolize the years when the Israelites lived in tents on the desert after the exodus.

The *sukkas* are decorated with fruits and vegetables of the harvest such as apples, pears, corn,

squash and pumpkin. (In the United States, cranberries are often used, too.) The roofs of the *sukkas* are covered with branches, but spaces are left between them so that the sky can be seen. All meals are eaten in the *sukka* unless it rains.

The last day of *Succoth*, called *Simchat Torah*, marks the end of the reading of the *Torah*. (*Torah* is the Hebrew name for the first five books of the Bible.) After the last lines are read, the *Torah* scroll is re-rolled to begin another cycle of reading. This cycle has been continuous for more than 3,000 years.

Simchat Torah is a joyous time. The *Torah* scroll is carried around the synagogue, followed by a parade of children carrying flags.

A special treat for *Simchat Torah* is candied apples on a stick.

CANDIED APPLES (*Parve*)   *Help

INGREDIENTS: ASSEMBLE AND MEASURE
6 large McIntosh apples (washed)
1 cup sugar
3/4 cup water
1/16 teaspoon cream of tartar
red food coloring

UTENSILS: ASSEMBLE
1 double boiler with lid
1 measuring cup
1 large metal spoon
1 candy thermometer
wax paper
sticks
oil to grease wax paper

WHAT TO DO

Cook	{ sugar / water / cream of tartar }	in top of double boiler over low flame. Make sure there is water in the bottom pot.
Stir	until dissolved	
Add	a few drops of red food coloring	
Cover	pot	
Bring	to a slow boil for 3 minutes	
* Insert	mixture in pot on top of double boiler	
* Keep	hot (300°) with medium flame. Test mixture with candy thermometer.	
Insert	sticks into the middle of the core of the apples	
Grease	wax paper	
* Dip	apple on stick into pot with syrup	
Remove	apple from pot to greased wax paper	
Let stand	until outside is hard	

Serves 6

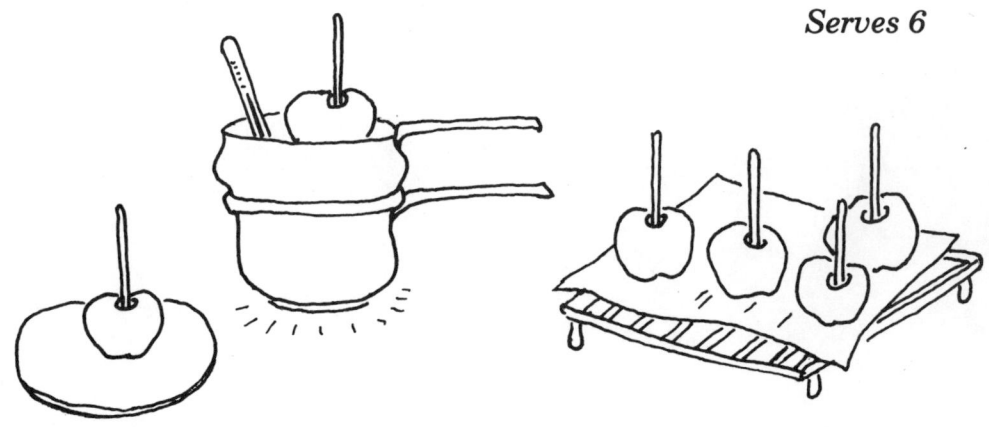

Hanukkah

Hanukkah, the Festival of Lights, is an eight-day celebration of the victory of Judah Maccabee and his brothers over their Syrian enemies.

When the victorious Maccabees reclaimed the Holy Temple in Jerusalem, they prepared to relight the *Menorah*. However, they found only one day's supply of sanctified oil. A miracle occurred! This little bit of oil burned for eight days—long enough to prepare a new supply.

To symbolize this miracle and victory, *Hanukkah* is celebrated by lighting the *Menorah*—one light for each day until the eighth day when all the lights are burning. The *Menorah* contains a ninth candle which is used to light the others.

It is easy to imagine that foods fried in oil are traditional *Hanukkah* dishes, especially potato pancakes (*latkes*) with applesauce.

POTATO PANCAKES (*Parve*)

INGREDIENTS: ASSEMBLE AND MEASURE	UTENSILS: ASSEMBLE
6 medium potatoes (washed)	1 vegetable peeler
1 medium onion	1 grater
3 eggs	1 measuring cup
¼ cup *matzoh* meal	1 set measuring spoons
1 teaspoon salt	1 large bowl
¼ teaspoon pepper	1 metal spatula
oil for frying	1 large frying pan
	paper towels

WHAT TO DO

Peel	potatoes	
Keep	potatoes in cold water until used. In this way, they won't turn black.	
Grate	{ potatoes, onion }	on fine side of grater
Mix	{ potatoes, onions, eggs, *matzoh* meal, salt, pepper }	thoroughly
Heat	oil in frying pan	
Drop	1 heaping tablespoon of potato mixture into frying pan. Repeat until mixture is finished.	

Fry	on both sides (turn when edges look brown)
Remove	from pan with spatula
Drain	on paper towels
Serve	hot with applesauce

About 14 pancakes

APPLESAUCE (*Parve*)

This is a delicious dish to eat with potato pancakes and wonderful, as a dessert, all by itself.

INGREDIENTS: ASSEMBLE AND MEASURE
8 cooking apples (washed)
1 cup sugar
1/8 teaspoon salt
2 teaspoons lemon juice
water to cover apples

UTENSILS: ASSEMBLE
1 knife
1 measuring cup
1 set measuring spoons
1 large saucepan with cover
1 sieve or ricer

WHAT TO DO

Slice	apples	
Put	apples in saucepan and barely cover with water	
Simmer	apples until soft	
Put	through sieve or ricer	
Return	to pot	
Add	⎧ sugar ⎨ salt ⎩ lemon juice	
Simmer	about 10 minutes	
Remove	from heat	
Serve	hot or cold	
Store	covered in refrigerator	

Serves 4

Tu Bi-Shevat

Tu Bi-Shevat is Arbor Day in Israel. It is a holiday dedicated to the trees. In a country like Israel, where the land is mostly desert, trees are very important. They hold the soil and prevent it from blowing away. They provide shade and lumber. Some trees bear fruit.

In Israel, all the children plant trees on *Tu Bi-Shevat,* the New Year of the Trees. They are given little bags of fruit and nuts to wear around their necks.

Traditional foods native to the land of Israel are served to commemorate this day. These are foods such as oranges, dates, figs, almonds and *bokser* or carob, a kind of fruit.

BAKED APPLES (*Parve*)

INGREDIENTS: ASSEMBLE AND MEASURE
6 large Rome Beauty baking apples (washed)
1/3 cup sugar
1 teaspoon cinnamon
1/3 cup raisins
1 cup water

UTENSILS: ASSEMBLE
1 knife
1 apple corer
1 set measuring spoons
1 measuring cup
1 pyrex baking dish 9" x 13"

WHAT TO DO

Preheat	oven to 350°
Remove	cores from apples
Peel	apples 1/3 of the way down
Arrange	apples in baking dish
Put	raisins into hole where core was removed
Sprinkle	{ sugar cinnamon } over apples
Pour	1 cup of water into bottom of baking dish
Bake	at 350° for 1 hour
Remove	from oven
Serve	hot or cold
Store	covered in refrigerator

Serves 6

Purim

*Once there was a wicked, wicked man
And Haman was his name, sir.
He would have vowed to murder all the Jews,
Though they were not to blame, sir.*

*Oh, today we'll merry, merry be
Oh, today we'll merry, merry be
Oh, today we'll merry, merry be
And nosh some hamantashen.*

*Esther was the lovely, lovely queen
Of King Ahasuerus
When Haman said he'd kill us all,
Oh my, how he did scare us.*

(Repeat refrain)

*When Esther speaking to the king
Of Haman's plot made mention,
"Ha ha," he said. "Oh no, he won't,
I'll spoil his bad intention."*

(Repeat refrain)

These verses are part of a song Jewish children sing on *Purim*. They tell about a tale which happened many, many years ago in ancient Persia. In those days, there was an evil prime minister named Haman who plotted the destruction of the Jewish community. He cast lots (for example, taking chances by pulling numbers out of a hat) to see on which day this horrible deed would be done.

Mordecai, the Jewish leader who was also the uncle of Queen Esther, found out about Haman's plan. He told the Queen, and she revealed the deadly plot to her husband, King Ahasuerus. They turned the tables on Haman who was disgraced and finally doomed. Mordecai became prime minister and the Jews were saved.

Today, over 2,500 years later, *Purim* is still celebrated. When the Scroll of Esther, the *Megillah*, is read in the synagogue, the mention of Haman's name is drowned out by loud foot-stamping and the sound of *groggers* (noisemakers) to symbolically stamp out all the evil in the world.

People bring gifts of fruit and sweets to their friends. They also give money to charity so everyone can enjoy the holiday. A favorite treat on *Purim* is a pastry called *hamantashen* which resembles the three-cornered hat worn during the time the story took place.

HAMANTASHEN (*Parve*, if *parve* margarine is used)

These three-cornered pastries are made of cookie dough. They are filled with either poppy seeds, chopped apricots with honey, chopped dates, jams, nuts, raisins, lekwar (prune concentrate), or various fruits.

INGREDIENTS: ASSEMBLE AND MEASURE
4 cups all-purpose flour
2 teaspoons baking powder
$1/2$ teaspoon salt
1 cup sugar
1 teaspoon vanilla
3 eggs
$1/3$ cup butter or margarine
$1/3$ cup orange juice
flour for rolling dough
butter or margarine for greasing cookie sheets
filling

UTENSILS: ASSEMBLE
1 set measuring spoons
1 set measuring cups
1 large bowl
1 small bowl
1 electric mixer
1 rubber spatula
1 knife
1 metal spatula
1 round cookie cutter or 1 large glass
1 rolling pin
1 rack
1 (or 2) cookie sheets
wax paper

WHAT TO DO

Sift	{ flour / salt / baking powder
Cream	butter or margarine in electric mixer
Mix	sugar with butter or margarine
Add	{ eggs / vanilla / orange juice } to sugar mixture
Add	flour mixture to sugar mixture gradually
Knead	dough until smooth

Roll out dough with rolling pin on floured surface until it is very thin, about $1/4''$ thick

Cut circles of dough using cookie cutter or rim of glass

Spread 1 teaspoon of filling in the middle of the circle

Shape into triangles (*See diagram*)

Preheat oven to 350°

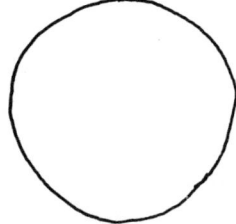

1. Cut out circle of dough.

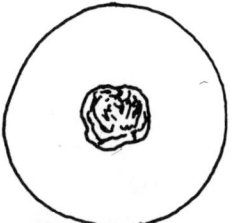

2. Put 1 teaspoon of filling in center of circle.

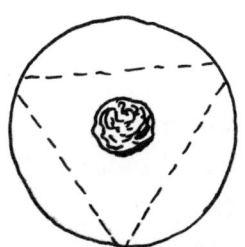

3. Fold up three sides to make a triangle, and pinch the sides together.

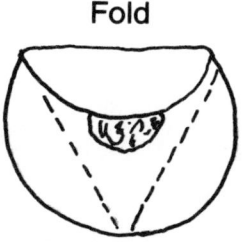

Fold

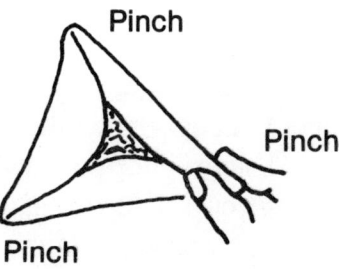

Pinch

Pinch

Pinch

Grease	cookie sheets
Arrange	*hamantashen* on cookie sheets 1" apart
Bake	in 350° oven for 20 minutes until lightly browned
Remove	from oven
Remove	from cookie sheet with metal spatula
Cool	on rack
Serve or	
Store	in closed container

                                    About 3 dozen hamantashen

BROWNIES (*Parve*, if *parve* margarine is used instead of butter)

INGREDIENTS: ASSEMBLE AND MEASURE
4 ounces unsweetened chocolate
½ cup butter
2 eggs
1 cup sugar
1 teaspoon vanilla
½ cup chopped walnuts
½ cup + 2 tablespoons all-purpose flour
½ teaspoon salt
butter for greasing pan

UTENSILS: ASSEMBLE
1 set measuring spoons
1 set measuring cups
1 electric mixer
1 rubber spatula
1 medium knife
1 9" x 9" baking dish
1 rack
1 large bowl
wax paper

WHAT TO DO

Preheat	oven to 350°	
Fill	bottom of double boiler half-way up with water	
Melt	{ butter chocolate }	in top of double boiler
Beat	{ eggs sugar }	in electric mixer
Add	{ chocolate mixture vanilla }	to egg mixture
Blend in	{ flour salt }	to chocolate-egg mixture
Stir	nuts into mixture	
Grease	pan	
Spread	wax paper in pan and up sides	
Grease	wax paper	
Spread	batter evenly over pan	
Bake	in 350° oven on middle rack about 25 minutes	
Cool	in pan	
Remove	from pan	
Remove	wax paper	
Cut	into squares or rectangles	
Serve or Store	wrapped individually in foil or plastic	

Makes about 24 to 30 brownies

Passover (Pesach)

Over 3,000 years ago, in ancient Egypt, the Jewish people were the slaves of the Egyptian pharaoh. As slaves, their lives were difficult until Moses led them out of Egypt and across the Sinai Desert to the Promised Land. (This is the area we now call the Holy Land.) This exodus is the theme of the Passover celebration, which expresses the love of freedom.

The holiday begins with the *seder*, a ceremonial dinner which follows a special order of blessings, eating of symbolic foods, and retelling the Passover story as it is written in the *Haggadah*.

The *seder* plate has five different foods on it. The lamb bone represents the lamb which was a special Passover sacrifice. The hard-boiled egg is a holiday offering from ancient times. *Maror*, or bitter herbs, recalls the sufferings of the Jews under the pharaoh. *Charoset*, symbolizes the mortar and bricks which the Jewish slaves made for the pharaoh's buildings. *Karpas*, or greens, represent spring, the time of year during which this holiday falls.

Passover has its own special foods which are served throughout the holiday. One of these is unleavened bread called *matzoh*, a flat sheet of dough made without yeast. Yeast is added to bread to make it rise. But the Jews left Egypt in such a hurry that they had no time for their bread to rise.

Bread and grains, as well as some other foods, are not allowed at any time during the eight days of

Passover. Such foods are called *chametz*. For this reason, matzoh meal and potato starch are used in cooking.

MAROR (*Parve*)
(Bitter Herbs)

INGREDIENTS: ASSEMBLE
1 horseradish (washed)
1 large piece romaine lettuce (washed)

UTENSILS: ASSEMBLE
1 medium knife
1 vegetable peeler
1 grater
1 bowl

WHAT TO DO

Remove	the ends of the horseradish
Peel	horseradish with peeler so outer layer is removed
Grate	horseradish into bowl
Serve	immediately or it tends to turn black. Place on a piece of romaine lettuce on the *seder* plate.

CHAROSET (*Parve*)

INGREDIENTS: ASSEMBLE AND MEASURE
2 large or 3 medium apples (washed)
½ cup chopped walnuts
¼ cup wine
½ teaspoon cinnamon

UTENSILS: ASSEMBLE
1 medium knife
1 measuring cup
1 chopper
1 wooden bowl
1½ teaspoon measuring spoon

WHAT TO DO

Peel	apples	
Cut	apples into pieces, removing and discarding core	
Chop	{ apples, nuts }	into tiny pieces
Mix in	{ wine, cinnamon }	until well blended
Serve or		
Store	in refrigerator	

For 8-10 peop

KARPAS (*Parve*)
(Greens)

INGREDIENTS: ASSEMBLE
lettuce, celery, or parsley

UTENSILS: ASSEMBLE
1 knife
paper towels

WHAT TO DO

Wash	greens thoroughly in cold water
Dry	with paper towels
Tear or cut	greens into small pieces so each person can have a few pieces

LAMB BONE

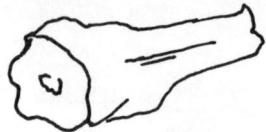

INGREDIENTS: ASSEMBLE
1 lamb bone (can be obtained from a *kosher* butcher)

UTENSILS: ASSEMBLE
1 small pan
1 pair tongs

WHAT TO DO

Turn	oven to broil
Place	lamb bone in pan under broiler
Broil	until brown
Turn	lamb bone over to brown on other side
Remove	from oven when brown
Serve	on *seder* plate

HARD-BOILED EGGS (*Parve*)

Hard-boiled eggs are good at any time. At the *seder*, they are dipped in salt water, then eaten. The egg on the *seder* plate is hard-boiled, then roasted in the oven.

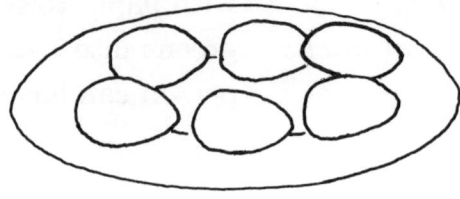

INGREDIENTS: ASSEMBLE
6 eggs at room temperature
water to cover

UTENSILS: ASSEMBLE
1 saucepan large enough so all the eggs can be covered with water
1 small baking pan
1 pair tongs

WHAT TO DO

Place	eggs in saucepan
Add	cool water to cover
Simmer	15 minutes over low heat
Let stand	for 5 minutes
Remove	from heat
Pour	cold water over eggs—it makes them easier to peel
Remove	eggs from water
Cool	eggs
Store	in refrigerator until they are used. Do not peel until they are used.

For the Seder Plate

Broil	egg in pan under broiler
Turn	with tongs
Remove	from oven
Serve	on *seder* plate

6 eggs serves 6

POTATO PUDDING (*Parve*)

During Passover, this pudding or *kugel* is made with *matzoh* meal; at other times, it can be made with flour.

INGREDIENTS: ASSEMBLE AND MEASURE
6 medium potatoes (washed)
1 medium onion
3 eggs
1/3 cup *matzoh* meal
1 teaspoon salt
1/2 cup oil
oil for greasing baking dish

UTENSILS: ASSEMBLE
1 potato peeler
1 grater
1 egg beater
1 measuring cup
1 set measuring spoons
2 bowls
1 9" x 9" baking dish

WHAT TO DO

Preheat   oven to 350°

Peel   potatoes. Keep in bowl of cold water until they are to be used otherwise they turn black.

Peel   onion

Grate   potatoes and onion on fine side of grater

Beat   eggs until thick

Mix   { potatoes, onion, eggs, *matzoh* meal, salt, oil } thoroughly

Grease	baking pan
Pour	mixture into baking dish
Bake	in 350° oven for 1 hour until golden brown
Serve	hot
Store	covered in refrigerator (may be reheated once)

Serves 4 to 6

MATZOH BALLS (*Parve*) *Help
(Knaidlach)

Knaidlach is the Jewish word for *matzoh* balls. Made with *matzoh* meal, they are light and fluffy, and are served in chicken or beef soup.

INGREDIENTS: ASSEMBLE AND MEASURE
1 cup *matzoh* meal
2 tablespoons oil
2 tablespoons cold water
2 eggs
1/2 teaspoon salt
water or soup for cooking

UTENSILS: ASSEMBLE
1 measuring cup
1 set measuring spoons
1 large bowl
1 fork
1 large wooden spoon
1 slotted spoon
1 large pot

WHAT TO DO

Beat	eggs with fork
Mix in	{ oil, water, salt, *matzoh* meal } until blended

73

Refrigerate	for about 20 minutes
Form	mixture into balls (wet hands with cold water for each ball)
* Lower	each ball gently into chicken or beef soup or boiling water to which 1 tablespoon of salt has been added. Use a slotted spoon.
Cook	30 to 40 minutes over medium heat
Remove	from soup with slotted spoon to soup plate. Pour soup into soup plate and serve hot.

About 16 matzoh balls

MATZOH BRIE (*Parve,* if made with *parve* margarine)
(Fried *Matzoh*)

This is a popular dairy dish which is usually served during Passover, but it is good at any time of the year. While this recipe calls for sugar and cinnamon, *matzoh brie* may also be served with salt and pepper.

INGREDIENTS: ASSEMBLE AND MEASURE
3 whole *matzohs*
3 eggs
½ teaspoon salt
water
½ teaspoon cinnamon
sugar to taste
2 tablespoons butter or margarine

UTENSILS: ASSEMBLE
1 set measuring spoons
1 fork
1 bowl
1 colander
1 pancake turner
1 large frying pan

WHAT TO DO

Break	*matzohs* into small pieces	
Put	*matzoh* in colander	
Pour	hot water over *matzoh*	
Drain	*matzoh*	
Beat	eggs in bowl with fork	
Mix	{ *matzoh* / salt / cinnamon }	with eggs
Melt	butter or margarine in frying pan	
Pour	egg-*matzoh* mixture into frying pan	
Brown	on both sides	
Serve	hot, sprinkled with sugar	

Serves 2 to 3

SPONGE CAKE (*Parve*)

INGREDIENTS: ASSEMBLE AND MEASURE
6 eggs
1 1/3 cups sugar
1/2 cup hot water
1 lemon (washed)
1/2 cup potato flour
1/2 cup *matzoh* cake meal
1/2 teaspoon salt
oil and flour for pan

UTENSILS: ASSEMBLE
1 set measuring spoons
1 set measuring cups
1 sifter
2 bowls
1 grater
1 rubber spatula
1 electric mixer
1 10" tube pan
1 rack
1 toothpick

WHAT TO DO

Preheat	oven to 325°
Grate	lemon rind on fine side of grater
Squeeze	lemon to extract juice
Separate	egg yolks from egg whites
Beat	{ egg yolks / sugar } together
Mix	{ lemon juice / lemon rind / hot water } with egg mixture
Sift	{ potato flour / cake meal } together
Mix	flour mixture with egg mixture
Beat	egg whites with salt until stiff
Fold	egg whites into batter

Grease and flour	bottom of baking pan
Pour	batter into pan
Bake	in 325° oven on middle rack for 1¼ hours (until toothpick inserted in cake comes out clean)
Remove	cake from oven
Invert	cake on wire rack to cool completely
Remove	from pan
Serve or Store	in closed container

Makes a 10" tube cake

ALMOND MACAROONS (*Parve*)

INGREDIENTS: ASSEMBLE AND MEASURE
1 cup almond paste
1 cup confectioners' sugar
3 egg whites
½ teaspoon vanilla
¼ cup shredded coconut

UTENSILS: ASSEMBLE
1 measuring cup
1 set measuring spoons
1 spoon
1 rack
1 knife or chopper
1 medium bowl
1 cookie sheet
wax paper
1 fork

WHAT TO DO

Preheat	oven to 325°
Cut	almond paste into small pieces
Add	sugar
Blend	with fingers or fork
Mix	egg whites in slowly and thoroughly
Mix	{ salt, vanilla, coconut } into almond-egg mixture
Cover	cookie sheet with wax paper
Drop	dough from teaspoon onto cookie sheet; cookies should be 1″ apart
Bake	in 325° oven on middle rack for 20 minutes
Remove	from oven
Cool	on rack
Remove	cookies from waxed paper
Serve or	
Store	in tightly covered container

About 36 macaroons

Independence Day

For thousands of years, the Jewish people have regarded a little piece of land at the eastern shore of the Mediterranean Sea as their home. First it was called Canaan when Abraham and Sarah settled there over 5,000 years ago. After many years, it was called Palestine. In 1948, under a United Nations Agreement, it became the nation of Israel.

This little piece of land, which is mostly desert, has been conquered and ruled by foreign countries innumerable times, but Jews have always lived there. Sometimes the invaders were repelled, and sometimes they were not. Nevertheless, to the Jews, both in Israel and in other countries, this land was always their home. In it lies their roots and the origin of their history.

At the beginning of this century, while the Turks and the British ruled Palestine, a great number of Jews began to settle there. They worked hard to reclaim the desert and make it bloom.

It was not until 1948, after World War II, that the United Nations agreed to grant Israel independence. On May 15, 1948, when word of independence reached Israel, there were shouts of joy and dancing in the streets. At last there was a Jewish homeland. Every year, Jews from all over the world celebrate Israeli Independence Day.

While native Israeli cooking includes dishes of many countries, Middle Eastern cooking is the most popular. The following recipes are native to the Middle East and are typically Israeli. For this reason, they are served to celebrate Independence Day.

HUMMUS (*Parve*) *Help

Hummus is usually served with *pita* (a bread with a pocket). This appetizer, which originated in the Middle East, is becoming popular in the United States.

INGREDIENTS: ASSEMBLE AND MEASURE
2 cups chick peas (washed)
2/3 cup *tahina*
1/4 cup lemon juice
2 cloves garlic
1 teaspoon salt
1/8 teaspoon black pepper
1 tablespoon chopped parsley (washed)
water

UTENSILS: ASSEMBLE
1 measuring cup
1 set measuring spoons
1 medium bowl
1 knife
1 colander
1 medium pot with cover
1 thin rubber spatula
1 electric blender

WHAT TO DO

Soak	chick peas covered with water overnight
Rinse	chick peas
Cook	chick peas in water (make sure they are covered with water) in covered pot for 2 and 1/2 hours, until tender
Drain	in colander
Peel	garlic

*Blend { cooked chick peas / garlic / lemon juice / salt / pepper / *tahina* } in a blender until smooth

Chop   parsley
Garnish   with parsley
Serve   cold with pita
Store   in refrigerator

Serves 6 to 8

TAHINA (*Parve*)

Tahina is a paste made from sesame seeds and water. Although it is sold in stores which carry Middle Eastern foods, nowadays, many supermarkets stock it, too.

INGREDIENTS: ASSEMBLE AND MEASURE
1 cup *tahina*
2 cloves garlic
½ cup water
1 teaspoon salt
3 tablespoons lemon juice
8 black olives } optional
4 sprigs parsley (washed) }

UTENSILS: ASSEMBLE
1 medium knife
1 garlic press
1 medium bowl
1 wooden spoon
1 measuring cup
1 set measuring spoons

WHAT TO DO

Peel	garlic
Squeeze	garlic through press
Mix	{ tahina, garlic, water, salt, lemon juice } until creamy
Garnish	with parsley and olives (optional)
Serve	on individual plates or in a bowl as a sauce for *falafel*
Store	in refrigerator

Serves 4 to 6

FALAFEL (*Parve*)

This popular Israeli dish is served in *pita* (a bread with a pocket). In Israel, it is sold on street corners the way hot dogs are sold in the United States.

INGREDIENTS: ASSEMBLE AND MEASURE	UTENSILS: ASSEMBLE
2 cups chick peas	1 measuring cup
2 tablespoons flour	1 set measuring spoons
1/2 teaspoon baking soda	1 slotted spoon
1 clove garlic	1 large wooden spoon
1 teaspoon salt	1 garlic press
1/4 teaspoon pepper	1 knife
1/8 teaspoon chili pepper	1 food grinder
1 egg	1 medium bowl
oil for deep frying	1 large bowl
water	1 deep fryer (pot)
	1 colander
	paper towels

WHAT TO DO

Soak	chick peas covered with water overnight
Drain	in colander
Grind	chick peas in food grinder
Peel	garlic
Squeeze	through garlic press

	⎧ ground chick peas ⎫	
	⎪ garlic ⎪	
	⎪ egg ⎪	
Mix	⎨ flour ⎬ *thoroughly*
	⎪ baking soda ⎪	
	⎪ salt ⎪	
	⎪ pepper ⎪	
	⎩ chili pepper ⎭	

Heat	oil in deep fryer
Form	mixture into small walnut-sized balls. Dip hands into cold water for each ball.
*Drop	the balls into the hot oil CAREFULLY
Fry	until golden brown
*Remove	from oil with slotted spoon
Drain	on paper towels
Serve	in *pita* with cole slaw or salad and *tahina*
Store	in refrigerator, may be reheated

About 12 to 16 balls depending on size

KIBBUTZ SALAD (*Parve*)

In Israel there are plenty of fresh vegetables. For the past 50 to 60 years, the settlers have irrigated the desert so that many kinds of fruits, vegetables and flowers can grow there. All the ingredients in this salad are grown in Israel—the land that was mostly desert.

On a *kibbutz,* all the salad vegetables are frequently served in one large bowl. Each person helps himself or herself, cutting up the vegetables and then adding the dressing.

INGREDIENTS: ASSEMBLE AND MEASURE
2 large tomatoes
1 large cucumber
1 large green pepper
4 scallions
6 radishes
6 large, pitted black olives
1 teaspoon salt
1/4 teaspoon pepper
1/4 cup oil
2 tablespoons vinegar
1 teaspoon lemon juice

UTENSILS: ASSEMBLE
1 set measuring spoons
1 measuring cup
1 knife
1 cutting board
1 large fork and spoon
1 small bowl
1 large bowl
1 small spoon

WHAT TO DO

Wash   all vegetables thoroughly

Cut   all vegetables into bite-sized pieces
        tomatoes
        cucumber
        green pepper
        scallions
        radishes
        olives

Mix	{ salt, pepper, oil, vinegar, lemon juice }	thoroughly in small bowl
Toss	salad with dressing using large fork and spoon	
Serve	cold immediately	
Store	in refrigerator, although it tastes best when served immediately	

Serves 4 to 6

PITA (*Parve*)   *Help

This is a flat, round bread that is Middle Eastern in origin. Its two sides form a pocket which can be stuffed with various foods like tuna fish or *falafel*.

INGREDIENTS: ASSEMBLE AND MEASURE
2 packages dry yeast
1/2 teaspoon sugar
2 cups warm water
1/2 cup oil
1 tablespoon salt
6 cups unbleached all-purpose flour
oil to grease bowl
cornmeal to spread on baking sheet

UTENSILS: ASSEMBLE
1 set measuring spoons
1 measuring cup
1 set measuring cups
1 large bowl
1 rolling pin
1 medium wooden spoon
1 cloth (dish cloth)
2 baking sheets
1 rack

WHAT TO DO

Dissolve	$\left\{\begin{array}{l}\text{yeast}\\ \text{sugar}\\ \text{1/2 cup warm water}\end{array}\right\}$ in bowl
Let stand	for 10 minutes
Add	$\left\{\begin{array}{l}\text{1 and 1/2 cups water}\\ \text{oil}\\ \text{salt}\\ \text{flour (gradually)}\end{array}\right.$
Mix	above ingredients thoroughly
Put	dough on lightly floured flat surface
Knead	about 10 minutes until smooth and elastic
Form	into ball
Grease	large bowl
Put	dough into bowl, turn over so it is completely covered with oil
Cover	with cloth
Let rise	about 2 hours until doubled in bulk. Keep in a warm place.
Punch	down dough
Divide	into 9 balls
Let rise	about 1/2 hour
Sprinkle	corn meal on baking sheets
Preheat	oven to 500°
Roll	each ball into a circle on a lightly floured surface

Put	circles on baking sheets
* Place	baking sheet with pita on lowest rack of oven for 5 minutes. Pita will puff up like a small balloon when it is in the oven. It deflates as it cools.
* Transfer	sheet to highest rack for 2 to 3 minutes
Remove	from oven
Cool	thoroughly on rack
Serve	stuffed with desired ingredient
Store	wrapped in plastic as soon as cooled

Makes 8 to 9 loaves

Shavuot

Exactly seven weeks after the second Passover *seder* comes the holiday of *Shavuot*. This is the time when God gave the *Torah* to the Jews at Mt. Sinai. Before this event, the laws of *kashruth* (separation of meat and dairy) were unknown. Therefore, it has become a tradition to eat dairy foods during this holiday.

Shavuot is also called the "Festival of the Fruits." It is the time of late spring when the first fruits and vegetables are harvested. For this occasion, many homes and synagogues are decorated with flowers and greens.

BUTTER

INGREDIENTS: ASSEMBLE AND MEASURE
1 pint of cold, heavy, sweet cream
1 pinch of salt (optional)

UTENSILS: ASSEMBLE
1 bowl
1 egg beater
  OR
1 jar with lid that fits tightly

WHAT TO DO

Pour	cream into bowl
Add	salt (optional)
Beat	with egg beater until cream turns to butter
or Pour	cream into jar, then cover tightly
Shake	until cream turns to butter

Serve or

Store in refrigerator or can be tightly wrapped and stored in freezer

WHIPPED CREAM

INGREDIENTS: ASSEMBLE AND MEASURE
1 pint of heavy, sweet cream (cold)
2 tablespoons of confectioners' sugar

UTENSILS: ASSEMBLE
1 bowl
1 egg beater
1 measuring spoon—tablespoon
1 large metal spoon

WHAT TO DO

Pour cream into bowl

Whip with egg beater until cream makes soft peaks

Fold in sugar

Serve cold as a topping for fruits, cakes, puddings, ice cream

Store covered, in refrigerator

About 4 cups whipped cream

EGG SALAD (*Parve*)

INGREDIENTS: ASSEMBLE AND MEASURE
6 hard-boiled eggs
1 stalk celery (washed)
3 tablespoons mayonnaise
1 teaspoon salt
1/4 teaspoon pepper

UTENSILS: ASSEMBLE
1 set measuring spoons
1 knife
1 bowl
1 cutting board
1 large spoon

1 slice onion (medium)
1 teaspoon prepared mustard
paprika

WHAT TO DO

Peel	hard-boiled eggs
Dice	{ eggs celery onion slice
Mix	{ salt pepper mustard mayonnaise } together
Combine	{ eggs onion celery mayonnaise mixture
Garnish	with paprika
Serve	in a bowl or spread on sandwiches
Store	covered, in refrigerator

Serves 3

TUNA FISH (*Parve*)

INGREDIENTS: ASSEMBLE AND MEASURE
1 6½ ounce can white meat tuna
1 slice onion
1 stalk celery (washed)
3 tablespoons mayonnaise
2 teaspoons lemon juice

UTENSILS: ASSEMBLE
1 can opener
1 knife
1 fork
1 medium bowl
1 cutting board

WHAT TO DO

Drain	oil from can of tuna
Flake	tuna with fork
Dice	{ celery { onion
Mix	{ tuna { celery { onion } thoroughly { mayonnaise { lemon juice
Serve	cold on a bed of lettuce or spread on sandwiches
Store	covered in refrigerator 1 day

Serves 2

RICE PUDDING

INGREDIENTS: ASSEMBLE AND MEASURE
1½ cups cooked white rice**
3 cups milk
3 eggs
½ cup sugar
⅛ teaspoon salt
1 teaspoon vanilla
1 tablespoon butter
½ cup seedless raisins
butter or oil for greasing baking dish

UTENSILS: ASSEMBLE
1 medium saucepan with cover
1 measuring cup
1 set measuring spoons
1 medium bowl
1 large bowl
1 egg beater
1 large mixing spoon
1 baking dish (3 quart casserole)

WHAT TO DO

**Follow directions on package since there are many different kinds of white rice on the market and each may have its own instructions for cooking.

Transfer	rice to large bowl
Beat	eggs with egg beater
Melt	butter in saucepan
Add	eggs, milk, melted butter, sugar, vanilla, salt, raisins } to rice
Stir	thoroughly
Preheat	oven to 325°
Grease	baking dish
Pour	mixture into baking dish
Bake	in 325° oven on middle rack one hour (until set)
Remove	from oven
Serve	warm or cold
Store	covered in refrigerator

Serves 6

CHEESECAKE

INGREDIENTS: ASSEMBLE AND MEASURE

CRUST
16 graham crackers (squares)
1/3 cup sugar
1/3 cup melted butter
butter to grease pan

FILLING
2 8-ounce packages cream cheese
1 1/2 cups sour cream
2 eggs
1/2 cup plus 1 tablespoon sugar
2 teaspoons vanilla
2 teaspoons lemon juice
2 tablespoons melted butter

UTENSILS: ASSEMBLE
1 measuring cup
1 set measuring spoons
1 small saucepan
1 small bowl
1 large bowl
1 mixing spoon
1 rubber spatula
1 electric mixer
1 9" spring form pan
1 rolling pin
wax paper

WHAT TO DO

CRUST	*Put*	crackers between 2 sheets of wax paper and roll over them with rolling pin to make crumbs
	Melt	1/3 cup butter in saucepan
	Mix	{ butter sugar cracker crumbs
	Grease	springform pan
	Line	springform pan with crumb mixture on bottom and 1/3 up the side of pan; press down to form a shell
	Chill	for 15 to 20 minutes in refrigerator

FILLING

Cream	cream cheese in electric mixer
Melt	butter (2 tablespoons)
Beat in	sugar thoroughly
Beat in	eggs thoroughly
Add	{ vanilla sour cream lemon juice melted butter
Blend	all ingredients thoroughly
Preheat	oven to 340°
Pour	cream cheese mixture into crumb-lined pan
Let stand	10 to 15 minutes
Bake	in 325° oven on middle rack for 50 minutes
Turn	oven off
Leave	cake in oven for 1 more hour
Remove	cake from oven
Cool	completely
Refrigerate	for at least 8 hours before serving
Serve	remove side of spring form pan, slide knife under cake, transfer to plate
Store	in refrigerator

Makes a 9" cheesecake

LEMONADE (*Parve*)

Lemonade has been a popular drink since the 14th century. It is very popular in Israel. Oranges can be substituted for lemons to make orangeade.

INGREDIENTS: ASSEMBLE AND MEASURE
7 lemons (washed)
   (1 to be sliced)
6 tablespoons super-fine sugar
1½ quarts water
ice cubes
mint leaves (washed)

UTENSILS: ASSEMBLE
1 juicer
1 knife
1 measuring cup
1 measuring tablespoon
1 strainer
1 large spoon
1 large pitcher

WHAT TO DO

Cut	{ 6 lemons in half { 1 lemon into 6 slices
Squeeze	lemon halves on juicer
Strain	lemon juice to remove pits
Add	sugar to lemon juice in pitcher
Add	{ water { ice
Stir	lemonade
Garnish	{ with mint leaves { lemon slices
Serve	ice cold
Store	in refrigerator

Serves 6